Team Spirit

THE TAMPA BAY RAYS

BY

MARK STEWART

Content Consultant
James L. Gates, Jr.
Library Director
National Baseball Hall of Fame and Museum

NORWOOD HOUSE PRESS
CHICAGO, ILLINOIS

Norwood House Press
P.O. Box 316598
Chicago, Illinois 60631

For information regarding Norwood House Press, please visit our website at:
www.norwoodhousepress.com or call 866-565-2900.

All photos courtesy of Getty Images except the following:
Topps, Inc. (14, 21 both, 29, 34 top, 35 top left, 37, 43);
Skip Milos/Rays (15); Tampa Bay Rays (39); Matt Richman (48 top).
Cover: Courtesy of the Tampa Bay Rays
Special thanks to Topps, Inc.

Editor: Mike Kennedy
Designer: Ron Jaffe
Project Management: Black Book Partners, LLC.
Special thanks to Ellen Beesley and Jeff Macolino.

Library of Congress Cataloging-in-Publication Data

Stewart, Mark, 1960-
    The Tampa Bay Rays / by Mark Stewart ; content consultant, James L.
Gates, Jr.
        p. cm. -- (Team spirit)
    Summary: "Presents the history, accomplishments and key personalities of
the Tampa Bay Rays baseball team. Includes timelines, quotes, maps, glossary
and website"--Provided by publisher.
    Includes bibliographical references and index.
    ISBN-13: 978-1-59953-175-5 (library edition : alk. paper)
    ISBN-10: 1-59953-175-5 (library edition : alk. paper) 1. Tampa Bay Devil
Rays (Baseball team)--History--Juvenile literature. I. Gates, James L. II.
Title.
GV875.T26S74 2008
796.357'640975965--dc22
                                                          2007043498

Manufactured in the United States of America.

3701

COVER PHOTO: The Rays celebrate an exciting victory in 2008.

Table of Contents

SPORTS WORDS & VOCABULARY WORDS: In this book, you will find many words that are new to you. You may also see familiar words used in new ways. The glossary on page 46 gives the meanings of baseball words, as well as "everyday" words that have special baseball meanings. These words appear in **bold type** throughout the book. The glossary on page 47 gives the meanings of vocabulary words that are not related to baseball. They appear in ***bold italic type*** throughout the book.

Meet the Rays

The sports world is full of fun stories about teams that find the *formula* for success and rise to capture a championship. During a season, however, most teams struggle—and only one team can win it all. The Tampa Bay Rays know this as well as anyone.

Since joining the **American League (AL)** in 1998, the Rays have made important strides. Although victories were often hard to come by, the team never lost its spirit. Tampa Bay plays each game to win. When other teams take them lightly, the Rays usually *seize* the opportunity. That attitude gives fans a reason to cheer their team and come to the ballpark.

This book tells the story of the Rays. They have some of baseball's most talented and exciting players. More important, those players are focused on winning. When they walk onto a baseball field, they believe they can beat anyone.

The Rays congratulate each other after a win in 2008.

Way Back When

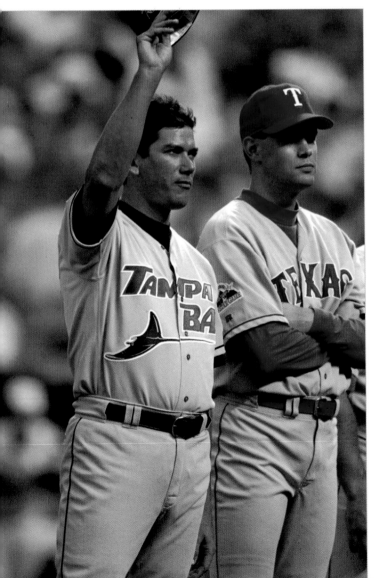

In March 1995, the owners of **Major League Baseball**'s 28 teams voted to add two new clubs for the 1998 season. One team was the Arizona Diamondbacks. The other was the Tampa Bay Devil Rays. Tampa Bay is located on the west coast of Florida. It is home to the cities of Tampa and St. Petersburg. The team's stadium, Tropicana Field, was built in St. Petersburg.

The owners of the Devil Rays paid $130 million for their team. At the time, it was the highest price ever for a baseball club. One of the *investors* was a company called Home Shopping Network. Another was a businessman named Vincent Naimoli. He was the man most responsible for bringing a team to the area.

Naimoli had grown up rooting for the Brooklyn Dodgers as a boy. Like many New Yorkers, he was heartbroken when the team moved to California in 1958. Forty years later, Naimoli had his own baseball team. The Rays—the team's new name starting in 2008—joined the **AL East**. It was a strong division with several powerful teams.

Tampa Bay fans knew they would have to be *patient* while the Rays built a *competitive* club. They were amazed when the team won 12 games in its first month in 1998. No **expansion team** had ever done that well. In May, the Rays swept four games from the Baltimore Orioles in Camden Yards, the Orioles' home park. Baltimore had been the AL East champion the year before.

The Rays began with players who were unwanted by other teams. That group of **veterans** included Roberto Hernandez, Wilson Alvarez, Fred McGriff, Miguel Cairo, and John Flaherty. Tampa Bay also signed Rolando Arrojo, a pitcher who came to the United States from Cuba. He was the first Ray to *represent* the team in the **All-Star Game**.

LEFT: Rolando Arrojo waves to the fans at the 1998 All-Star Game.
ABOVE: Fred McGriff, Tampa Bay's first great home run hitter.

The team added more ***experienced*** stars in the years that followed. Among the Rays best known by fans were Wade Boggs, Jose Canseco, Vinny Castilla, Greg Vaughn, and Steve Trachsel. They had all been All-Stars earlier in their careers.

Meanwhile, the Rays were also busy signing and developing young **prospects** to lead the team into the future. The fans kept close track as Julio Lugo, Aubrey Huff, Toby Hall, Randy Winn, Victor Zambrano, Rocco Baldelli, and Carl Crawford worked their way toward the major leagues and into the Tampa Bay **lineup**. In 2004, the team won 12 games in a row and finished in fourth place in the AL East. After that performance, the decision to go with young players became very easy.

Through smart spending and ***shrewd*** trades, the Rays have been able to stick to their plan of building their team with youthful stars. As Tampa Bay moved into the 21st ***century***, its talent continued rising to the top. With a new ***generation*** of stars taking over, the Rays gave their fans a glimpse of the team's future—and showed it was definitely worth the wait.

LEFT: Carl Crawford, one of the most exciting players in Rays history.
ABOVE: Rocco Baldelli gives a high five to Aubrey Huff as he crosses home plate after a home run.

9

The Team Today

After relying on older players for many years, the Rays decided to let the "kids" play. In 2007, they had the youngest starting lineup of any team in baseball. The fans were thrilled when prospects B.J. Upton, James Shields, and Jonny Gomes showed they could be stars in the big leagues. Scott Kazmir, a hard-throwing pitcher, was the AL's strikeout leader. Veteran players such as Carlos Peña, Akinori Iwamura, and Al Reyes also made important contributions.

The Rays have promised Tampa Bay a winning team. They have young stars to build around, and their fans are eager to watch championship baseball. It is not easy to compete with strong AL East teams such as the New York Yankees and Boston Red Sox. The Rays face many challenges.

To begin a new era in Tampa Bay baseball, the team announced big changes starting in 2008. Among other things, the team officially changed its name to the "Rays." The uniforms the Rays wear have a different look, too. The team introduced new colors and a new *logo* for 2008.

Evan Longoria is greeted by excited teammates after a home run in 2008.

Home Turf

The Rays play in a domed stadium that was built in 1990. It was first called the Suncoast Dome, and then renamed the Thunder Dome. Later it became Tropicana Field. The stadium was built with the hope that the Chicago White Sox would move there. When that did not happen, the Tampa Bay Lightning hockey team moved in. When the Rays finally arrived in 1998, the stadium was remodeled to feel more like an old-time ballpark.

One of the unusual things about the Rays' stadium is that it has walkways that hang from the ceiling. High fly balls that hit these "catwalks" are in play. In a 2006 game, Jonny Gomes belted a ball that landed on a catwalk and slowly rolled off. Gomes had already touched third base and was headed home when the shortstop caught the ball. The umpire called Gomes out.

BY THE NUMBERS

- *The Rays' stadium has 45,000 seats.*
- *The distance from home plate to the left field foul pole is 315 feet.*
- *The distance from home plate to the center field fence is 404 feet.*
- *The distance from home plate to the right field foul pole is 322 feet.*

The lighted catwalks can be seen at the top of the Rays' stadium.

Dressed for Success

For their first 10 seasons, the Rays used green and black as their main team colors. Their caps had the letters *TB* for "Tampa Bay" and showed a swimming manta ray (also called a devil ray). Their jerseys said either *Tampa Bay* or *Devil Rays* across the front.

When Tampa Bay switched its name from Devil Rays to Rays, the change was made on the team's uniforms, too. It was the first time in more than 40 years that a team took a new name without moving to another city. The Houston Colt .45s did the same thing in 1965 when they became the Astros.

Tampa Bay's uniforms are more colorful than they used to be. The

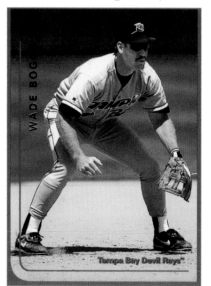

team replaced its familiar green and black with a combination of dark blue, light blue, and gold. The team's new logo shows a baseball diamond and a sunburst. The team still features a swimming ray as part of its logo, but there is a new focus in Tampa Bay. The club wants fans to also think of sunny beaches when they see the name Rays.

Wade Boggs in Tampa Bay's uniform from 1998.

UNIFORM BASICS

The baseball uniform has not changed much since the Rays began playing. It has four main parts:

- a cap or batting helmet with a sun visor
- a top with a player's number on the back
- pants that reach down between the ankle and the knee
- stirrup-style socks

The uniform top sometimes has a player's name on the back. The team's name, city, or logo is usually on the front. Baseball teams wear light-colored uniforms when they play at home and darker styles when they play on the road.

For more than 100 years, baseball uniforms were made of wool *flannel* and were very baggy. This helped the sweat *evaporate* and gave players the freedom to move around. Today's uniforms are made of *synthetic* fabrics that stretch with players and keep them dry and cool.

Carl Crawford wears the team's 2008 home uniform.

We Won!

The first victory for a new team is always exciting. The players have only been together a short time. The fans are just becoming familiar with the players. No one knows who the heroes will be. No one knows when that first win will come.

In the Rays' very first game in 1998, they played the Detroit Tigers at home. More than 45,000 fans jammed into the stadium. Their *enthusiasm* dropped a little when their team fell behind 11–0, but they continued cheering for their Rays. Tampa Bay came back to score six runs but still lost.

The next night, around 30,000 fans settled into their seats to watch a rematch between the two teams. The Tigers built a lead again, scoring three times in the top of the first inning. This time, the Rays struck back right away. They scored twice in the bottom of the first to make the score 3–2.

Starter Rolando Arrojo settled down and began pitching well for the Rays. In the fourth inning, Tampa Bay sent nine batters to the plate and scored four runs. Miguel Cairo got the hit that put the Rays ahead for the first time in their history. Wade Boggs, Fred McGriff, and Rich Butler also drove in runs.

The Tigers kept the game close. The score was 7–6 in the seventh inning when Butler hit a home run to give Tampa Bay an 8–6 lead. The Tigers scored in the following inning, but once again the Rays bounced back. In the bottom of the eighth, McGriff drove two runners home with a single—his third and fourth **runs batted in (RBI)** of the game—and

LEFT: The Rays and the Detroit Tigers line up before Tampa Bay's first game.
ABOVE: Wade Boggs shakes hands with baseball legend and Florida resident Ted Williams before the Rays take the field against the Tigers.

Dave Martinez hit a single to make the score 11–7.

Roberto Hernandez came into the game for the Rays in the ninth inning to protect the lead. He allowed one run, and then the Tigers put two more runners on base. Hernandez took a deep breath and peered in for the catcher's signals. He struck out Joe Oliver and got Frank Catalanatto to lift a harmless pop fly for the third out. The Rays had their first win.

It was an exciting victory that was close until the final out. Arrojo—one of eight **rookies** on the team—earned the win, but it was the Tampa Bay hitters who were the stars of the game. They drilled 18 hits off of six Detroit pitchers and scored runs when the team needed them most.

ABOVE: Rolando Arrojo delivers a pitch. **RIGHT**: Fred McGriff, one of the hitting stars for the Rays in their first victory.

Go-To Guys

To be a true star in baseball, you need more than a quick bat and a strong arm. You have to be a "go-to guy"—someone the manager wants on the pitcher's mound or in the batter's box when it matters most. Fans of the Rays have had a lot to cheer about over the years, including these great stars …

THE PIONEERS

FRED McGRIFF   First Baseman

• BORN: 10/31/1963   • PLAYED FOR TEAM: 1998 TO 2001 & 2004

Fred McGriff was Tampa Bay's first star **slugger**. He grew up in the area and loved playing in front of his friends and family. In 1999, he hit .310—his best batting average ever. Twice with the Rays, he drove in more than 100 runs.

ROBERTO HERNANDEZ   Pitcher

• BORN: 11/11/1964   • PLAYED FOR TEAM: 1998 TO 2000

Roberto Hernandez was one of the finest **relief pitchers** in baseball when he arrived in Tampa Bay. He showed why in the Rays' second season. The team only won 69 games, but Hernandez came in and **saved** 43 of those victories.

ABOVE: Roberto Hernandez
TOP RIGHT: Toby Hall   **BOTTOM RIGHT**: Aubrey Huff

TOBY HALL   Catcher

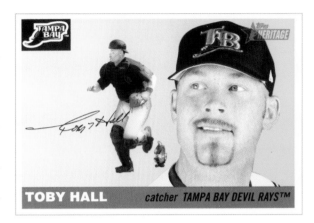

- BORN: 10/21/1975
- PLAYED FOR TEAM: 2000 TO 2006

Toby Hall was a good hitter and a solid defensive catcher. The Tampa Bay fans loved him for his hard play—and also for the "soul patch" on his chin. Hall would dye the tuft of hair different colors to mark different occasions.

TOBY HALL   catcher TAMPA BAY DEVIL RAYS™

AUBREY HUFF   Infielder/Designated Hitter/ Outfielder

- BORN: 12/20/1976
- PLAYED FOR TEAM: 2000 TO 2006

The Rays **drafted** Aubrey Huff in 1998, and he soon became Tampa Bay's most dangerous power hitter. In his career with the team, Huff hit 128 homers and had two seasons with more than 100 runs batted in.

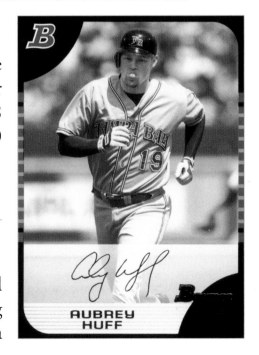

AUBREY HUFF

JULIO LUGO   Shortstop

- BORN: 11/16/1975
- PLAYED FOR TEAM: 2003 TO 2006

The Rays signed Julio Lugo hoping he could plug holes in the lineup while their young players gained experience. Instead, he became a star. In 2005, Lugo hit .295 and stole 39 bases.

MODERN STARS

CARL CRAWFORD   Outfielder

• BORN: 8/5/1981   • FIRST YEAR WITH TEAM: 2002

Carl Crawford could have been a basketball guard or football quarterback. In fact, he turned down offers in both sports when he agreed to play for the Rays. Crawford quickly became the team's most exciting player. He led the AL in stolen bases in 2003, 2004, 2006, and 2007.

SCOTT KAZMIR   Pitcher

• BORN: 1/24/1984   • FIRST YEAR WITH TEAM: 2004

The Rays made one of the best trades ever when they got Scott Kazmir during the 2004 season. Very few left-handed pitchers ever threw as hard as he did. In 2007, he led the AL in strikeouts.

B.J. UPTON   Outfielder/Infielder

• BORN: 8/21/1984   • FIRST YEAR WITH TEAM: 2004

The Rays expected B.J. Upton to be their shortstop of the future. In 2007, they moved him to center field, and he became a star at his new position. Upton was one of only six players in the AL to hit more than 20 home runs and steal 20 bases that season.

JAMES SHIELDS   Pitcher

• BORN: 12/20/1981   • FIRST YEAR WITH TEAM: 2006

James Shields was the first Tampa Bay pitcher to start his career with four wins in a row. He could strike out batters with two different fastballs and a sneaky **changeup**. In 2007, he won 12 games and led the team in innings pitched.

AKINORI IWAMURA   Third Baseman

• BORN: 2/9/1979   • FIRST YEAR WITH TEAM: 2007

The Rays signed Japanese star Akinori Iwamura to be their third baseman. He had few problems making the *transition* to his new team. In 2007, Iwamura batted .285 and led the Rays with 10 triples.

CARLOS PEÑA   First Baseman

• BORN: 5/17/1978   • FIRST YEAR WITH TEAM: 2007

Carlos Peña had a *remarkable* year in his first season with Tampa Bay. He set team records with 46 home runs and 121 runs batted in. Peña showed the young Rays what it takes to have a great season.

LEFT: B.J. Upton
TOP RIGHT: James Shields
BOTTOM RIGHT: Carlos Peña and Akinori Iwamura

On the Sidelines

Experience is everything when it comes to managing a baseball team. The Rays have always looked for managers with great knowledge of baseball. The team's first **skipper** was Larry Rothschild. As a coach with the Cincinnati Reds and Florida Marlins in the 1990s, he had helped both clubs win championships. Rothschild was known for being very patient with Tampa Bay's young players.

Hal McRae and Lou Piniella, by contrast, were not known for their patience. They demanded hard work and smart decisions from their players. Both had a burning desire to win when they were players, and they were the same as managers with Tampa Bay.

In 2006, the Rays hired Joe Maddon to manage the team. Maddon had been working with young players as a coach in the AL for more than 30 years. Under Maddon, Tampa Bay's next generation of stars blossomed. He was easy to spot walking in the dugout with his thick black glasses. Some Tampa Bay fans liked to copy Maddon by wearing black glasses to Rays games.

Joe Maddon watches the action from the dugout.

One Great Day

Baseball fans had a lot to cheer about during August 1999. Mark McGwire hit his 500th home run on the 5th of the month, and Tony Gwynn stroked his 3,000th hit a day later. Wade Boggs of the Rays was not far behind Gwynn. On August 7th, he collected two singles in his first two **at-bats** against the Cleveland Indians to give him 2,999 hits for his career. The fans at Tropicana Field rose

to their feet when Boggs came to bat in the sixth inning. They wanted to see him make history.

Boggs did not disappoint them. He drove a curveball from Chris Haney over the right field wall for his 3,000th hit. He was the 23rd player to reach 3,000 hits but the first to get that number with a home run.

As Boggs rounded the bases, so many memories rushed through his mind. He had moved to the Tampa Bay area as a boy and grew up just

LEFT: Wade Boggs swings for his 3,000th hit.
RIGHT: Boggs acknowledges his hometown fans.

a few miles away from the Rays' stadium. He had also been a Little League star in Tampa.

Boggs thought about his mother, too. She had been killed in a car accident many years earlier. He pointed to the sky after rounding third base and then knelt down and kissed home plate before being congratulated by his teammates.

The baseball that Boggs hit was caught by a fan named Mike Hogan. He had just moved to Tampa. Hogan gave the ball to Boggs after the game. A few weeks later, Boggs injured his knee and decided to retire. He finished his career with 3,010 hits and a .328 batting average—one of the highest in history. Rays fans felt lucky for the opportunity to see him in a Tampa Bay uniform.

Legend Has It

Which record-smashing Ray started the 2007 season without a spot on the team?

LEGEND HAS IT that Carlos Peña did. At the end of spring training in 2007, the Rays told Peña that he was not playing well enough to make the club—he would have to go to the **minor leagues**. A last-minute injury to another player gave him a second chance—and he made the most of it. Peña won the starting job at first base and set team records for home runs, runs batted in, **slugging average**, and walks.

ABOVE: Carlos Peña
RIGHT: Fred McGriff

Who was the team's all-time hometown hero?

LEGEND HAS IT that Doug Waechter was. Waechter was a pitcher who grew up right in St. Petersburg. His friends and family were thrilled when he was drafted and signed by the team in 1999. Imagine how happy they were when Waechter started his first game for Tampa Bay in 2003—and gave up two hits and no runs in nine innings to the Seattle Mariners. Waechter was just the ninth AL pitcher since 1970 to throw a **shutout** in his first big-league start.

Which Ray provided the idea for a television series?

LEGEND HAS IT that Fred McGriff did. McGriff's nickname was "Crime Dog," and that was the title of a show proposed for TV. It was about a baseball player who secretly fought crime between games. The show never aired, but McGriff still has a script as a souvenir.

It Really Happened

D uring the 1980s, Jim Morris tried to make it to the big leagues as a pitcher. He played in the minor leagues for several seasons, but arm injuries kept him from achieving his dream. Morris finally became discouraged. He decided to become a physical science teacher at Reagan County High School near his home in Texas. He also coached the school's baseball team.

During one season in the late 1990s, Morris made a deal with his team. He promised he would give big-league baseball one more try if Reagan won the district championship. When the Owls took the title, Morris held up his end of the **bargain** and asked the Rays for a tryout. At first the team refused. Morris was 35 and had not pitched in many years. Then he threw 12 pitches at 98 miles per hour. Morris was as amazed as the Rays were. His arm had completely healed!

Tampa Bay signed Morris to a contract and sent him to the minor leagues. He pitched so well that the Rays added him to their roster in September 1999. Morris struck out the first batter he faced, Royce Clayton of the

Texas Rangers. He pitched in 21 games for Tampa Bay in 1999 and 2000 before his old arm problems returned.

Morris retired from baseball in 2001. One year later, a movie of his life was made. *The Rookie* starred Dennis Quaid as Morris. The movie was very popular and even won an ESPY Award as the top sports movie of the year in 2002. Morris now speaks at special events and still coaches baseball in Texas.

LEFT: Jim Morris fires a pitch for the Rays.
ABOVE: Dennis Quaid and Morris show off their ESPY Award.

Team Spirit

The Rays have put a lot of time and money into making games fun for their fans. There are party areas behind the **bullpens** in Tropicana Field, and a stingray tank sits behind the center field fence. Fans can actually touch the rays before the game. The ballpark's restaurants serve everything from steak to pizza to the famous Sting 'Em dog.

In 2006, the Rays opened the Ted Williams Museum and Hitters **Hall of Fame**. Williams was a Hall of Fame player for the Boston Red Sox and lived in Florida for much of his life. Anyone with a game ticket for the Rays gets into the exhibit for free.

Tampa Bay's team spirit is also kept high by the team *mascot*, a furry blue stingray named Raymond. After the Rays win, the entire Tampa Bay region shares in the celebration. The stadium roof glows bright orange so everyone in Tampa and St. Petersburg knows the Rays have earned a victory.

Toby Hall signs autographs for excited Rays fans.

Timeline

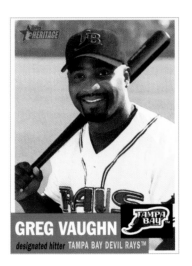

Greg
Vaughn

1998
The Rays play
their first season.

2000
Greg Vaughn leads the
team with 28 homers.

1995
Baseball owners
vote to add the
Rays to the AL.

1999
Wade Boggs slams
a home run for the
3,000th hit of his career.

2001
Hal McRae becomes
manager of the team.

Wade
Boggs

Hal
McRae

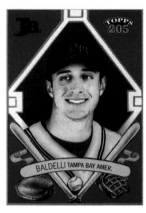

Rocco
Baldelli

Jorge
Cantu

2003
Rocco Baldelli leads all rookies with 184 hits.

2005
Jorge Cantu sets a team record with 117 runs batted in.

2006
The Rays finish with a winning record at home for the first time.

2008
The Rays play in their first World Series and lose to the Philadelphia Phillies.

2002
The Rays slug six home runs in a game against the Kansas City Royals.

2004
The team finishes fourth in the AL East.

2007
Carl Crawford blasts a home run in the All-Star Game.

Carl Crawford gets a high five after his All-Star Game home run.

Fun Facts

ROGER AND OUT

In 2001, the Rays beat Roger Clemens of the New York Yankees twice. He lost only one other game all year.

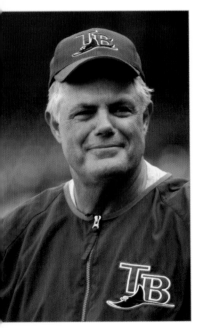

HAIR TODAY, BLONDE TOMORROW

During the 2003 season, 60-year-old manager Lou Piniella promised to bleach his hair if the Rays won three games in a row. When they did, Piniella showed up at the stadium the next day as a blonde.

THAT'S A NO–NO

In high school, Scott Kazmir pitched four **no-hitters** in a row. He missed a fifth by one out—and then pitched no-hitters in his next two games!

STORMY WEATHER

In September 2000, a game was postponed at Tropicana Field because of bad weather. It was just the third time that had ever happened at a domed baseball stadium.

ABOVE: Lou Piniella   **RIGHT**: Carl Crawford

MR. 200

During his years with the Rays, Fred McGriff became the second player ever to hit 200 homers in the AL and **National League (NL)**. The first player was Frank Robinson, a member of the Hall of Fame.

BETTER AND BETTER

Carl Crawford was only the second player in history to increase his batting average and home runs in each of his first five seasons. The first was Hall of Famer Rogers Hornsby.

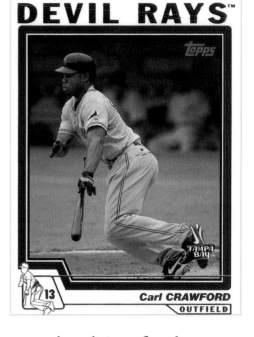

HAVE GLOVE, WILL TRAVEL

When Japanese star Akinori Iwamura signed with the Rays in 2007, he was not sure which position he would play for the team. Iwamura played it safe—he brought five different gloves to his first practice.

WHO'S THE BOSS?

B.J. Upton's initials stand for Bossman Junior. He got the nickname because of his father, who was known as Bossman. B.J.'s real name is Melvin.

Talking Baseball

"Even though things might not go the way you want, don't let any setbacks get in the way of your dreams."
—*Carlos Peña, on never giving up*

"I played the game one way— I gave it everything I had."
—*Wade Boggs, on the importance of hustling all the time*

"I want to be like the old-school guys. They played hard, and they played from the heart."
—*Carl Crawford, on why he always gives 100 percent*

"Let's do it intelligently, let's do it quickly, let's get it done, and then move on."

—Joe Maddon, on the right way to do baseball drills

"If I make an ***impression***, fine. I would be happy with that. But really, all that matters is winning."

—Akinori Iwamura, on what is most important in baseball

"The pitchers are much more in control. They can throw any variety of pitches on any given count."

—B.J. Upton, on the challenges of hitting in the big leagues

"You don't get the opportunity to build from the ground up in very many situations."

—Larry Rothschild, on why he was excited to be the team's first manager

"This is a dream for me; it really is—to be the leader of a staff going into the season."

—Scott Kazmir, on being named the Rays' number-one starting pitcher

LEFT: Carl Crawford
RIGHT: Scott Kazmir

For the Record

T he great Rays teams and players have left their marks on the record books. These are the "best of the best" …

RAYS AWARD WINNERS

WINNER	AWARD	YEAR
Rolando Arrojo	All-Star	1998
Jose Canseco	All-Star	1999
Roberto Hernandez	All-Star	1999
Fred McGriff	All-Star	2000
Greg Vaughn	All-Star	2001
Randy Winn	All-Star	2002
Lance Carter	All-Star	2003
Carl Crawford	All-Star	2004
Danys Baez	All-Star	2005
Scott Kazmir	All-Star	2006
Carl Crawford	All-Star	2007
Carlos Peña	Comeback Player of the Year	2007
	AL Pennant	2008

ABOVE:
Jose Canseco
RIGHT: Scott Kazmir
NEXT PAGE:
Carlos Peña

Pinpoints

The history of a baseball team is made up of many smaller stories. These stories take place all over the map—not just in the city a team calls "home." Match the pushpins on these maps to the Team Facts and you will begin to see the story of the Rays unfold!

TEAM FACTS

1 St. Petersburg, Florida—*The team has played here since 1998.*

2 Hazleton, Pennsylvania—*Joe Maddon was born here.*

3 Norfolk, Virginia—*B.J. Upton was born here.*

4 Woonsocket, Rhode Island—*Rocco Baldelli was born here.*

5 Marion, Ohio—*Aubrey Huff was born here.*

6 Omaha, Nebraska—*Wade Boggs was born here.*

7 Houston, Texas—*Scott Kazmir was born here.*

8 Petaluma, California—*Jonny Gomes was born here.*

9 Tacoma, Washington—*Toby Hall was born here.*

10 Havana, Cuba—*Rolando Arrojo was born here.*

11 Santurce, Puerto Rico—*Roberto Hernandez was born here.*

12 Ehime, Japan—*Akinori Iwamura was born here.*

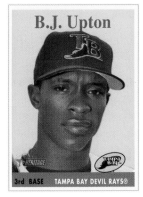

B.J. Upton

Play Ball

Baseball is a game played between two teams over nine innings. Teams take one turn at bat and one turn in the field during each inning. A turn at bat ends when three outs are made. The batters on the hitting team try to reach base safely. The players on the fielding team try to prevent this from happening.

In baseball, the ball is controlled by the pitcher. The pitcher must throw the ball to the batter, who decides whether or not to swing at each pitch. If a batter swings and misses, it is a strike. If the batter lets a good pitch go by, it is also a strike. If the batter swings and the ball does not stay in fair territory (between the v-shaped lines that begin at home plate) it is called "foul," and is counted as a strike. If the pitcher throws three strikes, the batter is out. If the pitcher throws four bad pitches before that, the batter is awarded first base. This is called a base-on-balls, or "walk."

When the batter swings the bat and hits the ball, everyone springs into action. If a fielder catches a batted ball before it hits the ground, the batter is out. If a fielder scoops the ball off the ground and throws it to first base before the batter arrives, the batter is out. If the batter reaches first base safely, he is credited with a hit. A one-base hit is called a single, a two-base hit is called a double, a three-base hit is called a triple, and a four-base hit is called a home run.

Runners who reach base are only safe when they are touching one of the bases. If they are caught between the bases, the fielders can tag them with the ball and record an out.

A batter who is able to circle the bases and make it back to home plate before three outs are made is credited with a run scored. The team with the most runs after nine innings is the winner.

Anyone who has played baseball (or softball) knows that it can be a complicated game. Every player on the field has a job to do. Different players have different strengths and weaknesses. The pitchers, batters, and managers make hundreds of decisions every game. The more you play and watch baseball, the more "little things" you are likely to notice. The next time you are at a game, look for these plays:

PLAY LIST

DOUBLE PLAY—A play where the fielding team is able to make two outs on one batted ball. This usually happens when a runner is on first base, and the batter hits a ground ball to one of the infielders. The base runner is forced out at second base and the ball is then thrown to first base before the batter arrives.

HIT AND RUN—A play where the runner on first base sprints to second base while the pitcher is throwing the ball to the batter. When the second baseman or shortstop moves toward the base to wait for the catcher's throw, the batter tries to hit the ball to the place that the fielder has just left. If the batter swings and misses, the fielding team can tag the runner out.

INTENTIONAL WALK—A play when the pitcher throws four bad pitches on purpose, allowing the batter to walk to first base. This happens when the pitcher would much rather face the next batter—and is willing to risk putting a runner on base.

SACRIFICE BUNT—A play where the batter makes an out on purpose so that a teammate can move to the next base. On a bunt, the batter tries to "deaden" the pitch with the bat instead of swinging at it.

SHOESTRING CATCH—A play where an outfielder catches a short hit an inch or two above the ground, near the tops of his shoes. It is not easy to run as fast as you can and lower your glove without slowing down. It can be risky, too. If a fielder misses a shoestring catch, the ball might roll all the way to the fence.

Glossary

BASEBALL WORDS TO KNOW

AL EAST—A group of American League teams that plays in the eastern part of the country.

ALL-STAR GAME—Baseball's annual game featuring the best players from the American League and National League.

AMERICAN LEAGUE (AL)—One of baseball's two major leagues; the AL began play in 1901 and the National League started in 1876.

AT-BATS—Turns hitting. "At-bats" are also a statistic that helps to measure how many times a player comes to the plate.

BULLPENS—The areas where a team's relief pitchers warm up; this word also describes the groups of relief pitchers in those areas.

CHANGEUP—A slow pitch disguised to look like a fastball.

DRAFTED—Selected at the annual meeting at which teams take turns choosing the best players in high school and college.

EXPANSION TEAM—A new team added to a league.

HALL OF FAME—The museum in Cooperstown, New York, where baseball's greatest players are honored. A player voted into the Hall of Fame is sometimes called a "Hall of Famer."

LINEUP—The list of players who are playing in a game.

MAJOR LEAGUE BASEBALL—The top level of professional baseball leagues. The American League and National League make up today's major leagues. Sometimes called the "big leagues."

MINOR LEAGUES—The many professional leagues that help develop players for the major leagues.

NATIONAL LEAGUE (NL)—The older of the two major leagues; the NL began play in 1876 and the American League started in 1901.

NO-HITTERS—Games in which a team is unable to get a hit.

PROSPECTS—Young players who are expected to become stars.

RELIEF PITCHERS—Pitchers who are brought into a game to replace another pitcher. Relief pitchers can be seen warming up in the bullpen.

ROOKIES—Players in their first season.

RUNS BATTED IN (RBI)—A statistic that counts the number of runners a batter drives home.

SAVED—Recorded the last out in a team's win. A pitcher on the mound for the last out of a close victory is credited with a "save."

SHUTOUT—A game in which one team does not allow its opponent to score a run.

SKIPPER—Another term for a manager.

SLUGGER—A powerful hitter.

SLUGGING AVERAGE—A statistic that helps measure a hitter's power. It is calculated by dividing the number of total bases a batter has by his official times at bat.

STARTER—The pitcher who begins the game for his team.

VETERANS—Players who have great experience.

46

OTHER WORDS TO KNOW

BARGAIN—Deal or agreement.

CENTURY—A period of 100 years.

COMPETITIVE—Having a strong desire to win.

ENTHUSIASM—Strong excitement.

EVAPORATE—Disappear, or turn into vapor.

EXPERIENCED—Having knowledge and skill in a job.

FLANNEL—A soft wool or cotton material.

FORMULA—A set way of doing something.

GENERATION—A period of years roughly equal to the time it takes for a person to be born, grow up, and have children.

IMPRESSION—Something pictured in the mind.

INVESTORS—People who spend their money for the purpose of making more money.

LOGO—A symbol or design that represents a company or team.

MASCOT—An animal or person believed to bring a group good luck.

PATIENT—Able to wait calmly.

REMARKABLE—Unusual or exceptional.

REPRESENT—Act, speak, or stand for something.

SEIZE—Capture or control.

SHREWD—Smart or clever.

SYNTHETIC—Made in a laboratory, not in nature.

TRANSITION—A change from one place to another.

Places to Go

ON THE ROAD

TAMPA BAY RAYS
One Tropicana Drive
Saint Petersburg, Florida 33705
(727) 825-3137

**NATIONAL BASEBALL
HALL OF FAME AND MUSEUM**
25 Main Street
Cooperstown, New York 13326
(888) 425-5633
www.baseballhalloffame.org

ON THE WEB

THE TAMPA BAY RAYS   www.tampabayrays.com
  • *Learn more about the Rays*

MAJOR LEAGUE BASEBALL   www.mlb.com
  • *Learn more about all the major league teams*

MINOR LEAGUE BASEBALL   www.minorleaguebaseball.com
  • *Learn more about the minor leagues*

ON THE BOOKSHELF

To learn more about the sport of baseball, look for these books at your library or bookstore:

  • Kelly, James. *Baseball*. New York, New York: DK, 2005.

  • Jacobs, Greg. *The Everything Kids' Baseball Book*. Cincinnati, Ohio: Adams Media Corporation, 2006.

  • Stewart, Mark and Kennedy, Mike. *Long Ball: The Legend and Lore of the Home Run*. Minneapolis, Minnesota: Millbrook Press, 2006.

Index

PAGE NUMBERS IN **BOLD** REFER TO ILLUSTRATIONS.

The Team

MARK STEWART has written more than 25 books on baseball, and over 100 sports books for kids. He grew up in New York City during the 1960s rooting for the Yankees and Mets, and now takes his two daughters, Mariah and Rachel, to the same ball-parks. Mark comes from a family of writers. His grand-father was Sunday Editor of the *New York Times* and his mother was Articles Editor of *Ladies' Home Journal* and *McCall's*. Mark has profiled hundreds of athletes over the last 20 years. He has also written several books about his native New York and New Jersey, his home today. Mark is a graduate of Duke University, with a degree in history. He lives with his daughters and wife, Sarah, overlooking Sandy Hook, NJ.

JAMES L. GATES, JR. has served as Library Director at the National Baseball Hall of Fame since 1995. He had previously served in academic libraries for almost fifteen years. He holds degrees from Belmont Abbey College, the University of Notre Dame, and Indiana University. During his career Jim has authored several aca-demic articles and has served in an editorial capacity on multiple book, mag-azine, and museum publications, and he also serves as host for the Annual Cooperstown Symposium on Baseball and American Culture. He is an ardent Baltimore Orioles fan and enjoys watching baseball with his wife and two children.